AQIQO

AND THE QUEST BEGINS...

ER. SONALI N

my dear friends, I am a blessed daughter of angels! my lovely parents Mr. Diwakar Yadav & Mrs. Asha Yadav have been a great influence in my life not only for being parents but for being my guide, inspiration, and teaching me to think out of the box! every moment I spend, every breath I take I miss them. I know they keep an eye on me from heaven. in my life, I did every possible thing to make them proud. my every success, all the achievements, awards, accolades, and my first book AQIQO I dedicate to my great parents and their unique upbringing style. always miss you mom and dad, lots of love your princess.

Contents

Foreword

Mr.Vinod M Bothale

I had an opportunity to meet Ms. Sonali in 2002 at one of the International conferences on geospatial technologies (Map Asia-2002). I was amazed to see her enthusiasm and zeal to learn something new and implement it by crossing all the odds.

During the past two decades, I could see Sonali achieve a series of successes in diverse not-so-common domains. Every time, she would appraise and surprise me with something new she had accomplished; quality operations and a Master's black belt in Six Sigma was the one that attracted me a lot and especially the application domains where she has applied it.

In her book, AQIQO, she narrated her journey of success in several projects, duly acknowledging the support, guidance, and mentorship she received from fellow colleagues. She is a great woman who has the robust capabilities of an initiator and leader who dreams of something and achieves it. Her book AQIQO is a fountain of energy and inspiration for many to achieve their dreams without losing hope.

The especially young generation will be able to get insights for achieving the targets and understand how their attitude, strategy & passion wins over the issues and hurdles.

I Congratulate Sonali and wish her for her future endeavors.

I am sure readers will enjoy the book.

Vinod M Bothale

Former, Associate Director & Outstanding Scientist

NRSC/ISRO

Preface

Life is the most beautiful gift we receive from God almighty, we all must count our blessings every day and

be grateful to the universe & all divine powers for blessing us in all possible ways.

once you start being grateful & thankful for your blessings you will receive more blessings. it's up to us to

fill out life with blessings & make it beautiful or keep complaining about what we don't have and make it painful to live.

In AQIQO, I will share the challenges and how I made my life blessed and abundant!

I'm sure you all will enjoy this journey with me.

Acknowledgements

It is said that behind every successful man there is a woman, here I proudly say behind my great success are my Family, Friends, and above all great Mentors from the Industry.

Gratitude to all for empowering me to be who I am today.

My achievements could have been incomplete without a strong support system. I take this opportunity to acknowledge my dear husband Shreyas & my Genius son Tanishk for supporting me always in every thick and thin of life and my struggles. Without their support, I could not even complete my first book AQIQO.

Nevertheless, my furry babies junior(labrador) and Casper (Tibetian Lhasa apso) are a fountain of love and energy who always boost my positivity.

CHAPTER ONE

WHO AM I?

By God's grace, I belong to a broad-minded family, the only daughter of lovely parents and little sister of two brothers, Avinash and Rahul. I was always guided and protected by them. Even today, my brothers are too attached and concerned about me, so once a little sis, always a little sis!

My family has the concept of equality of gender. I was raised with brothers thinking like all are the same. We all are engineers. I consider myself fortunate to get such a healthy and beautiful upbringing.

Gratitude to the universe and my family!

This healthy childhood made me believe in gender equality, thinking out of the box, pursuing passions, and being a good human being, ultimately an independent headstrong, kind heart woman as others consider me.

Why this book?

I genuinely feel whatever struggles and challenges I face being a woman in this male-dominated industry must share with everyone so that students, working professionals, and new budding engineers can be prepared for such situations.

Also, top decision-makers from management can take a friendly note to establish a better work environment for their staff.

Every human being has a different approach, attitude, mindset, skillsets, and ego. Some of us want fast success with less or close to no effort, do not, Here comes the necessity to indicate a **holistic approach** to quality in our life. Let it flow in your blood, let it be your habit, let it be your lifestyle & identity.

AQIQO-Always **Q**uality **I**n & **Q**uality **O**ut. If you desire the best, you have to put in the best efforts, there is no shortcut to success. It takes your sweat & blood to reach the top.

Nothing is easy nothing is free in this world.

CHAPTER TWO

STRUGGLES

I am grateful to the universe for my blessings as I strongly believe in counting blessings and not the problems, Here for students and all my female followers from civil engineering, I will share my struggles and challenges and how I overcame those. I genuinely believe AQIQO will help you understand your actual worth, and you will get motivated to achieve every success you deserve.

My first struggle started when I was trying to take admission into a degree course with civil engineering as my 30% choice selection despite being a merit student!

I was often told my percentile is eligible for computers or electronics, It's more suitable for girls. Why would you want to select civil engineering? Is there a mistake in form filling? I was surprised by this approach and explained to them how dearly I wanted to become a civil engineer "creator of the better future"!

I eventually got the admission and soon realized being a girl student in the 80s and 90s in this male-dominated field that no lady willingly goes into.

Further credit also goes to the highest level of fieldwork, tough challenges, and more challenging job profiles of any civil engineer in India.

Since childhood, my parents raised me with the freedom to choose the things I wanted, so I chose this field to be like my father, who was into govt. Services in the civil engineering field with his expertise in the Quality of structures. I used to love to see the structures like roads, bridges, and dams, leaving me amazed not only as beautiful creations, an essential part of the infrastructure development of the country but also the creativity and efforts of its creators are equally appreciable, my career plan was defined to be a civil engineer with Quality as mainstream, to do my bit in the development of our country. Multiple challenges could not break me down, and today I take pride in being the creator. Handling megastructure projects like metros, dams, tunnels, roads, flyovers, and nuclear power plants in challenging situations, the struggle starts being a lady. No one likes a lady in charge. When based on merit, experience, and skills, a woman gets the position, resistance starts, politics start so do non-cooperations

Welcome to the world of male dominance!

Firstly let me have a disclaimer that I am not underestimating anyone, neither I am saying all are bad in the world. AQIQO is a genuine & authentic sharing of what I faced in my career. Not necessarily everyone faces the same. so friends, going on sites after completion of a degree in early professional life was a funny start to the career I used to hear comments like, "what this girl knows?" "what this girl will do here ?" "what will she teach us !?" "such a small girl cannot handle a site!" one or two pieces of elderly advice I got - "beta, don't spoil your life on sites. Get married, live happily." every day it used to be a new challenge to supervise the site, check the Quality, raise concerns and ask for corrections. As I constantly get blindsided or back answered from the contractors, mistry- "since 20/30 years, we have been doing it the same way ...don't tell us what is wrong and proper ". I never gave up. I talked to their leaders and elderly gang members about the flaws and harmful effects on structure, then when make leader conveyed the same thing, changes happened.

Here I learned that my life & career in this industry aren't gonna be easy, but I was determined to take civil engineering as a career, I stood firm in every resistance, and every objection taken to my gender V/S work. My journey has even seen worse situations, making me think of quitting, but I didn't choose this because this was my choice. I am happy to fight for my existence in the profession. I thought, let's break every ice and be a guiding and inspiring for all ladies in my field and many more. We always need to make choices in our lives. You might have faced such discrimination in life at some or the other point. Those either can break you or make you Unbreakable!

CHAPTER THREE

CHALLENGES

Apart from resistance and criticism from others, I received support and guidance from my mentors in the starting stage. I feel fortunate to had & have great mentors in my life who inspired me to do my best and be the best version of myself. One of them was the incredible support I received at the KK. Wagh college of engineering, working as a lecturer in the civil department. As lecturer, I handled many students for theory, site work, practical, lab, and viva. Many students still remember me. Our students come and tell us that we have changed their approach towards life, attitude & thinking - it is a great feeling for me. The joy was more than money or any position. Teaching is a noble profession. I genuinely love learning and teaching. Learning keeps me alive & by teaching, you can inspire others. Rendering my services at symbiosis institute of operations management (SIOM) Nasik as a guest lecturer was a wonderful experience. Setting exam papers was out of a box experience for me.

While working as an office engineer, I learned multiple software. Here only, I explored my new potential of quick learning any software & fast speed of operations. Later on, I kept learning every new software made for any industry, including design software, detailing software, BIM, GIS, project management, Six Sigma related tools, etc. From 2005-to 2007, Six Sigma was not known in the civil industry. There was a misunderstanding that it's helpful in only manufacturing industries. When I learned the basics of Six Sigma, I found it applicable in every industry, so I did it in depth. I completed my black belt and started experiments to show the benefits of cost, time, and Quality .on. I successfully conducted live experiments, my work was greatly appreciated, and I was sponsored for my master's black belt by one of the employer's prothious engineering services. I will always be grateful to my ex-boss & management of the company for such great appreciation. In 2010, I became the civil engineering industry's first six sigma master implementer with a proven record of completed projects. Later on, we discovered I was India's first civil engineer implementing lean & six Sigma combinations. Handling resistance & stubborn people have become my skill set by now!

Quality everywhere, Quality in personal life, And professional life, I became a symbol of the Quality in industry.

I started getting the benefits of AQIQO. Always Quality Inputs create Quality Outputs, Became my life. It started running through my veins and Body! If one believes in excuses, there is no improvement and betterment. if you keep doing average things, you will set average results only. If you want to be successful, be a trendsetter, you have to think best and imagine out of the box.

During this quality journey, I met Mr.Mahesh Malpathak, who greatly inspired me for further enhancements in my career by being a lead auditor for Quality. with his guidance, I became IRCA certified lead auditor for quality management systems. I got impaneled with BSI for the same. After completing the required criteria, I was assigned independent audits of construction giants of India, and my horizon expanded! My Thanks to Mahesh and team BSI!

During visits of sites in early days of my career, it was a frequent indecent non-availability of toilets at sites. Working at the site full day landed me in awkward situations too. I had to find nearby hotels, restaurants, etc., to ease the case in such scenarios.

Once during an audit conducted by TUV, we were auditee on the Flyover site, and one single toilet too created a big struggle for me to attend nature's call. Sites were never habitual for any lady engineer, so no provision was ever considered. Many of the sites were in remote areas like Dhar/Chambal, Jammu & Kashmir, Rajasthan, Himalayas, Jharkhand, Uttrakhand, and many more.

while return journey from one site, our bus was attacked by dakoits, we somehow escaped with our lives.

I have faced raging temp from -4 to 58 degrees c so traveling from head office to the remote place - the site was always a challenge. I had to think for my safety as a lady & be alert everywhere. During Jammu-Kashmir's work, I was warned by many seniors about the conditions there and advised not to go. But my portfolio included all tunnels, dams, metros, nuclear power plants, etc. skipping sites was not an option.

On the early eve of our departure from Mumbai to Srinagar airport, it had a nearby bomb blast. Situations were too dangerous. The Delay of one day in booking flights saved our lives.

When I landed after a long road journey and reached our site at Katra. lovely mother nature, but not a single soul was visible except the project site. Not even a water bottle or anything to eat was available on our journey

So friends always carry emergency food, water, a first aid kit, and mosquito spray with you on such travels.

My gratitude to all the teams and management at HCC for being the best in the support system.

Mr.Arun Karambelakar (Ex-President HCC), My ex-boss, Mr. Avinash harde (VP), and Mr. Satish Kumar(CTO) were always there to support and motivate me. They are not only incredible human beings, my mentors who changed my life to be a better version of myself by facing challenges & overcoming those.

While working at MML3- UGC Mumbai metro project as QA in charge of the project, I must say I got complete support from my quality team, all dept. MMRC, GC-Maple, who not only respected me as a colleague but appreciated my work frequently.

Working at this position when my kid had emergencies, managing those was a big challenge as I was 1.5 hours away when he was hospitalized by the school and I received the call of emergency. My husband was in Dubai at that time for business meetings, so I had to make arrangements at the site for the planned work for the day & leave to attend to him.

My team, client, and project head, Mr. Kailas Nayak, supported me like a mountain - a great person who respects women and appreciates their efforts and work with dignity.

When one lives in a place like Mumbai, life is adventurous, happening, and quite uncertain at some times. It becomes part and parcel of our life. Twice I was badly stuck in floods & once in collapse. By god's grace reached home alive.

While enhancing your skills, always focus on risk management, know the risks, assess those & and mitigate them to progress ahead. Learn new techniques and tools every day and do your knowledge management suitable for your skills while you are performing, be aware of changes, address them successfully & be better than yesterday. If you stop learning, you will be dead, outdated & soon out of the market. If u don't change, you will become stagnant & you know, being stagnant stinks! So be alive, be continuous, and become the best of you each day! My friendly advice to all is never to compromise on your dreams, don't let yourself settle for less, set a new goal, put in your quality efforts, be honest with yourself, do your best, and success is yours. In my life so far, multiple times, I was pressurized and threatened by people, suppliers/vendors, clients, and sometimes even a few of my seniors for making adjustments, manipulations, and compromises in Quality. My answer was always a "NO."

I live by my principles of honesty, truth, and sincerity with full quality efforts & and no compromises can ever be made in it, whatever may come my way! Friends, design your path & live by it. Never compromise. Do it once, and you are stuck in a loop of repeating it never forget the principles of sequencing & management garbage in then garbage out (GIGO) and (QIQO) quality in and Quality out. Needless to say, quality outputs result in success

CHAPTER FOUR

HUNGER FOR SUCCESS

I hope now you might have defined " success " for you. If not, then please do so at the earliest.

It's your life, and you shall define goals for yourself, a destination you want to reach & steps on the path to success.!

Being responsible for your own life, we already learned in previous chapters.

if you want to be successful, there's a particular set of rules you must follow -

1) **Be clear**: decide what you want to achieve. It shall be based on your liking, passions, and expertise.

2) **Believe in yourself:** once you are clear about what to achieve, start believing that you can achieve it, you are worth it, and start the journey! Be the believer because nobody else will if you don't believe in yourself.

3) **Quality planning:** to make something happen, you must have a plan. How to proceed, how much time to devote

what skills shall you learn? Make your checklists & checkpoints to verify if you are doing enough or not.

4) **Quality input:** never blame your circumstances, and never complain about lack of resources. If you have enough potential, nothing can stop you from getting whatever you aim at. Be unstoppable and unshakeable in putting in your best efforts.

5) **Burning desire:** I do not believe in excuses but the efforts . have a burning desire in your heart. Do not let yourself rest unless you are progressing enough on the path you decided to move ahead on if your desires are strong, then even God helps you. Universal energies help you to make things happen. Use the tools of manifestation. Positive affirmations, the law of attraction to sharpen your desires & stay focused always.

6) **Mind, Body, and Soul:** always remember every human being is born with great potential. We just need to understand our self-worth & act accordingly. Combinations of mind-body & soul play an integral role in our life. The more positive energy you have, the more positive things get attracted to you. Never let any negativity touch you! Your thoughts, eyes, and ears must only get quality input that is positive things. Stop watching negative things, stop hearing negative things, and stop talking about negative things. Say no to the negativity around you. Start getting up early in the morning, talk to the universe, and get positive energies from the environment around you. Like fresh air, water, nature, etc., it will give you a heart full of joy. If you are energetic, you can work as per your plan and properly manage your time. I suggest daily meditation is a must to increase your focus & concentration.

7) **Quality efforts:** friends, whenever we work on our plans with good energy and good intentions in an entirely positive way, nothing can stop us. If you have any weaknesses, work on those, be updated, and be honest with yourself. Never let bad happen to you . be just. Raise your voice against injustice if needed. Never let yourself suffer or be the victim of anything many females/males are victims of sexual harassment at the workplace, discrimination, unfair practices, politics, and inequal criteria for the same position. Problems can be more than these. Always remember some laws can always help you. Never fall victim to anything. Stand firm. Put your all efforts, and do not be scared of anything, just like Einstein believed, failures can not stop you, but you know what is not serving the purpose, so change your approach & move ahead. AQIQO calls your soul always. Put your best quality efforts, challenge yourself for the subsequent betterment and get that quality version of you.

8) **AQIQO: It** never stops. Let it be your lifestyle, habits, and way of life, the flow in your blood because we all deserve the best. Start today! Never let the world say where u shall stop. You will decide where you want to stop or just keep going. One can always have the next target or next dream on the list to achieve after your first achievement is successful. And do not forget to celebrate your victories, every small victory matters. You deserve to appreciate yourself.

9) **Be the light:** after receiving your destinations, and achieving dreams, do not forget your roots or struggles. Be the light for others, guide people, help people dream, reach their goals, and never be a critic of people, as the world already has many. It will not only keep you humble and down

to earth but will enlighten you further. After all, life is a beautiful journey. Spread light and happiness around you. The most honorable achievement for someone is the hearts of the people they have won. The respect earned.

CHAPTER FIVE

WHAT KEEPS YOU GOING

Those who are willing to achieve new horizons in life always take care of themselves to be fit & energetic.

Start getting up early to spare quality time for yourself, meditation, yoga-exercise of your choice, breathing(pranayama) for a healthy lifestyle

watch your eating and sleeping habits. If the mind-body & soul remains in good alignment, you have half reached success.

Unhealthy lifestyles & habits impact your mental peace & fitness so stay away from them. Stay focused, stay tuned. All can face failures in whatever they are doing.do not stop, but do your swot(strength, weakness, opportunity, threat) analysis again. Find problems & eliminate those. Conditions may be unfavorable, be strong not to quit, not to give up, or else you can never achieve the destination.

Always be surrounded by positive people and mentors who guide you to be better. Never forget you are the creator of your life, no one else!

The First thing all shall keep in mind is the decision to be successful.

Many people will create hurdles to demotivate you and underestimate your potential. You shall always believe & trust yourself. Be competitive, be irrcplaceable! Increase and upgrade your skills & potential to such an extent that there will be no one like you. Constantly explore new technologies, industry trends, and advanced tools in your field/work areas and study those to be up to date, be better than before, and be different then others. Remember, our competition shall never be with others but being our best version shall be the focus. Never let your fighter spirit die. just like advertisements on TV" because fighters always win." so be the best of you always!

CHAPTER SIX

PROFESSIONAL JOURNEY

the day when we start thinking of some field, areas of work, or any opportunity; doesn't matter at what location at what time, give weightage to market demands, new fields. Think ahead of the present time or career for yourself and not for the sake of family or friends

it's your life & career. Select only the area which will make you happy while working. If you select your passion or liking as a career, that's the best!

I did the same thing. Since my childhood, I saw my father doing research & development in the construction industry at MERI & quality controls, so I developed a liking for immense structures & processes of construction. Until my schooling got over, I had a clear idea that I wanted to be a civil engineer and creator of my own future & infrastructures.

Similarly, do your own SWOT analysis & find out what you want to be. Where you want to see yourself. Do proper research for options available and choose which suits you best.

Students facing trouble paying fees may search for sponsorships, scholarships, NGOs, or even education loans. But don't let anything stop you from achieving your fundamental right, education.

Do everything possible and everything in your power to make your dreams come true. Never let your dreams die. Let them fuel you. As a fantastic personality once said, Dr. A.P.J Abdul kalam once said, "dreams are not those you see while sleeping, but it's something that does not let you sleep". Keep reading, listening, watching, and learning. Stay motivated and inspired. It will keep your morel high. Everyone deserves success and a good life. The only question is if you are willing enough to work for it. To earn it with your potential. Don't wait for anyone's approval. You don't need it. The most important thing everyone needs to understand is to remain calm in every situation . in our personal & professional life, so many situations bring us to panic. If we can stay calm, we can better deal with the situation than panic and make it worse. Learning is a never-ending process, and you should never stop learning. It's a process of a lifetime to keep us alive & fresh. Always keep learning new things, and cultivate your hobbies. Find what relaxes you and surges you with energy, satisfaction, and joy. When I completed my degree in civil engineering, I knew I won't be stopping here. I learned GIS (geographical information system) from Pune in 2000, when most people had no idea of GIS.

As I was always interested in advanced technologies, I opted for those to enhance my career. Doing India's first Govt. GIS project for Nasik municipal corporation was a fascinating experience. While working under the guidance of Rolta experts & resilient, I could learn a lot more to upgrade my skills. This proved very beneficial when I worked on the Navi Mumbai planning project. While working in the GIS field, I got a golden opportunity to represent KKW at the international level in " Map-Asia " 2002 in New Delhi. Here I got exposure to ISRO Experts and many experts from the world. After coming back from the conference, my mind was full of new horizons and things I wanted to achieve now new goals, and new milestones to set. So along with the position of GIS - the divisional head of the company (Anant access) launched the detailing segment. Here I got an opportunity to set the complete depth of steel detailing from scratch. Running this operation successfully at an international level gave me high expertise in global client management in 2004. For error-free performance, I learned the latest Six Sigma and lean Sigma tools from our clients. I immediately learned it and mastered it in our operations. In 2005, I became a Six-Sigma black belt & started implementing tools in our work as per client requirements.

Point to mention here, this was the period when rarely anyone knew Six Sigma and its benefits. In India, people had misunderstandings that it was only applicable to manufacturing industries and no other. After learning every minor detail, I was the first from the civil engineering industry who successfully implemented it & shown results in turn of belt quality, cost savings & time cycle reduction. the triad of CTQ (cost - time- quality) became my expertise. A new horizon to conquer! At prothious engineering services with the great support of top management, I implemented combinations of six Sigma & lean Sigma. Successfully for which I received a recommendation letter to do a master's further. Here, after completion of CTQ Targets, based on data in hand & reports from management, I received the highest accolade -Six Sigma master implementer in the year 2009-2011. I was officially India's first civil engineer who successfully implemented six sigma operations & achieved great values for employees. My journey in six Sigma has been very tough, challenging, and full of resistance & criticism. I never gave any weightage to anything insignificant as such. What made me more robust and successful was my burning desire to break through every wall in my path. And to achieve every peak in this journey.

Apart from six Sigma now, I have skillsets in project management, BIM, detailing, GIS, risk management, knowledge management, change management, business continuity & multiple industry software with a top speed of operations. Operational excellence became my identity, my expertise in the industry. Based on this, I was honored to get impaneled with BSI as an auditor for the quality management system. At BSI, my mentor Mahesh guided me to upgrade to new standards of the health & safety and environmental management system and complete the trio of QMS, EMS, and OHSAS (now OHSMS) best fit for any industrial audit. here I got to audit more than 500 clients, which included a variety of EPC, design, manufacturing, sports, educational institutes, consultants, and many more giants.

This rich experience has broadened my thought process and more options for combinations of operations to attain excellence. BSI always gives a fair chance to all & promotes good performance for career enhancement. In the year 2011, I started working for BSI. I am associated with them as a technical expert & QHSE lead auditor. My gratitude always remains to Mahesh and team BSI for being a significant driving force to unleash my real potential.

Further working on megaprojects of India at Hindusthan construction company, I could complete the transition of the whole system from ISO 9001- 2008 to ISO 9001-2015 in only 9 months which was appreciated by top management. We handled quality operations of projects from head office and had site audits at quarterly intervals. Out of all the total sites, I was responsible for 25 mega projects. My portfolio became 24,000CR. Every project was an engineering marvel & highly challenging. So traveling to those remote places, auditing sites, all departments, training for quality operations, etc. These were the main activities.

Here the work environment was always positive, and the company's rich culture, which is employees oriented, is highly appreciable. Working on underground projects challenged my real potential, which I always loved. The thrill of new challenges and the adventure and excitement of facing new challenges gave me a kick, as people say nowadays. When we solve the critical issue, tough challenges are overcome, the joy we get, the satisfaction, the adrenaline-filled surge of excitement of anticipation of what's next? That's what drives me. And for me, it's totally worth the risks. I've always been a workaholic person. I loved the new challenges life had ready for me every day and overcoming them. This exposure made me further sharpen my skills.

That is a significant reason why one of our clients, MMRC of Mumbai metro project (MML-3), demanded me to handle the whole project as a key-Quality person, which was happening for the first time in the history of the company as well as my life. After much consideration and meetings by top management (VP Mr.Harde, CTO Mr. Sharma) and my consent, I was officially given full charge of the Mumbai metro project for quality assurances as a key project person from the client-side. I was the first lady civil engineer handling this position of the project. While handling the quality and training department, the JSW cement seniors were fascinated by me and my work and appreciated my commitment to seeking the best Quality with zero compromises. Here also, the area was sensitive. Historically preserved buildings, water table availability, and many more challenges demanded the best risk management. Every day was thrilling and full of challenges to overcome. Troubleshooting became a core area of my quality operations.

With the help of the project team & guidance of project head Mr. Nayak, client MMRC & GC-Maple team, we successfully achieved ISO 9001-2015 certification in only six months which was a great challenge considering the number of challenges like depths, and location of sites together.

This development was appreciated by head office also . for the same Fastrack operation, we attempted the Guinness world record and cleared the preliminary round. On this site/project, the tremendous support of my team and other departments was appreciable. In my life, I met a wide variety of people, some discriminating against women & some having high regard for women. I must mention that with my gratitude toward project head Mr. Nayak, the client team of MMRC & GC-Maple always treated me with high regard and appreciation for my work.

Many advanced materials, machines, and technologies were used in this project. It was a unique and insightful experience for me. Which also helped me gain multiple golden-hearted friends and mentors to cherish in the future. We are still in contact to this day.

Further, in my professional journey, I managed quality operations for 75 projects at Kalpataru group company -JMC. At JMC, I handled the additional role of the management representative and chairperson of the POSH committee, risk management cell & SAP-HANA.

Risk - management cell & knowledge management vertical was assigned to me after management decisions which was an honor for me. Working at JMC was composed of multifaceted site audits, training activities, quality events, management review meetings, and significant tasks.

the vital part to mention here is business intelligence work, dashboard development, SharePoint - DMS portal design & development, contributions to developing chat tools - kalpataru digital assistance, and mobile apps for site engineers. I have a tremendous interest in artificial intelligence (AI) & robotic processes and the automation of systems. Here I got an excellent platform & guidance from my seniors like Dep. President Mr. Lalit Tiwari, Mr. Neil, Mr. Saxena, who always motivated me.

I'd like to advise everyone reading this book to never stops learning. Knowledge is an ultimate weapon, and keep sharpening it. Your journey is special and unique. If you possess an arsenal of skills that are unique to you and which others do not have, it ultimately makes you unique and ahead of others. Focus on what matters.

Now I own two business verticals, Revaan International, which looks after Opex, implementations, ISO training & certifications, and imports & exports consultation. The second vertical is Solace Wellness Solutions which focuses on Inner engineering & inner management. A holistic approach to life. My journey started in engineering and now also covers Inner engineering simultaneously.

I'm currently associated with three international bodies, multiple social activities, NGOs, PETA India, Save soil, and Balika Vidya. For purpose of my life is to help mankind animals & environment. And many more to do my tiny bit, which I owe to society and nature to make it prosper.

During flood relief operations solace adopted a village 'Pal' to help in every bit; adopted 10 Balika for their education. For my all work done I was awarded Women excellency & WEPA- 2021. Also being nominated to CE/CR awards of India.

CHAPTER SEVEN

INSPIRATION

My first mentor, was the late Shri D.M. Yadav, my father.He too was a civil engineer, and always guided me for being the best of me.

I was always fortunate to get good mentors in my life. And the names of those must be mentioned with the highest regard and gratitude as they made me what I am today - Brave, unstoppable, unshakeable, and unbreakable!

I dedicate my success to my mentors, who inspired and motivated me to push myself and do better every day in my professional life. Fountain of energy Prof. V.D. Barve, Prof. KS. Bandi, Prof. V.K. Patil,Prof. Kadve, Prof. Sewlikar, Prof. Varne, Prof. Kute, Prof. Jadhav, and Vadnere mam always supported me as an engineering student and later lecturer.

My mentor Mr. Mahesh Malpathak, from Team BSI, always inspired me to learn new standards.

Mr.Arun Karambelkar(Ex.President-HCC),Mr. Satish Kumar Sharma (Ex CTO-HCC)and Mr. Avinash Harde (Ex VP-HCC) guided me and helped me develop in the best way. Mr. Lalit Tiwari (Dept. President -JMC), Mr. S.K. Tripathi (CEO- JMC) and Mr. Neil (VP-JMC) were the ones who assigned me the most critical roles and believed in me to get the job done, and always motivated me.

I have been greatly influenced by Shri Sadguru, Master Akarshana (Eric Ho), and Dr. Krishna N Sharma (Ex Vice-chancellor-Kampala) in my spiritual journey.

In my forthcoming books, I'll be diving deeper into my spiritual journey.

Although watching me from heaven, my dear parents always inspired me to challenge my limits and surpass them to better myself. My brothers Avinash & Rahul are not only my brothers but my guide, friends, and philosophers. My husband Shreyas, My son Tanishk are always motivating me to do something new and challenging. Whenever I am on work-related tours, they happily manage our home and themselves in my absence.

My Family & friends are my great admirer & supporters. we can find inspiration in the tiniest of things and people, to strive hard to achieve success to fulfill our dreams. The most crucial factor always is self-commitment. Find your inspiration now, develop yourself, and chase your dreams.

CHAPTER EIGHT

BREAKTHROUGH

Covid - 19 pandemic worldwide has changed everyone's life and their approach towards it to an extent we never imagined. The uncertainty became a reality.

The whole world suffered. All of us have lost someone during this challenging time. May all those souls rest in peace. I lost my dear father!

During the pandemic, all the industries shifted to online means of work or, as we refer to, " Work from home."

This caused a surge of crises everywhere, at the same time opening gateways to new options. Online learning has become an essential part of our lives.

You must learn to adapt to the adverse conditions and push through to be on the top. Thinking out of the box, being limitless, and being unstoppable will help you grow in ways you never knew before.

CHAPTER NINE

STEPS TO SUCCESS

1) as we know, the first step starts from believing in yourself in your own strength, be the believer.

2) prepare for success and be ready for failure in case, learn from the failures and move ahead. Do not give up!

3) learn to forgive, do not carry any burden or garbage in your mind, and let go. Have a clean slate!

4) Maintain positivity in your life.

Apart from all that, do you ever feel unsatisfied no matter how much you achieve? It's never enough? The emptiness? The void inside you? The sinking feeling?

If you ever experience any of the above, it's time to seek spiritual help and find Solace.

CHAPTER TEN

And the Quest Begins ...

Eeven for me, the above questions yielded an answer quite similar to yours, 'Yes.'

it took me quite a while to find what was causing this feeling. The emptiness and the vacancy. My spiritual Gurus helped me find and eliminate the root cause of this feeling and find Solace by balancing the Mind, Body, and soul.

My spiritual journey leads me to find calmness, peace, and satisfaction. It helped me find answers to my quest, the purpose of my life, and how my happiness lies in helping others and helping them heal.

Today I am an internationally certified & registered Energy Healer. My journey has just begun. If you'd like to dive deeper into my spiritual awakening and journey and how you can also do it, stay tuned for my next book, **Divine Order(Powers Unleashed)**

I hope you, too, will achieve your dreams & journey towards success soon.

Let the quest begin ...

Upcoming Books Of Author

Coming soon,

1: Divine Order - Powers unleashed

2: Angels with Tail -

3: Hakunaa Mattata - happiness unlimited

Praise For Author

Mr.Arun Karambelkar

Dear Friends,

I saw Sonali, whom I know professionally from HCC, as a fountain of confidence and positive energy. She worked for the Quality assurance and Quality management system of HCC's 25 megastructure projects. As a Quality Auditor, her work has been commendable! She completed the transition of the quality system in merely 9 months for head office, and our sites, which was an example of her great commitment and competence.

I appreciate her positive attitude in dealing with challenges and has left a great impression.

Her first book AQIQO demonstrates a simple way to design a path toward one's destination and the process to achieve success. It's a must-read book for every engineering student, management professional, and working woman too.

She is the winner of two awards and her journey in the field of civil engineering is quite appreciable! My blessings and best wishes to her.

Arun Karambelkar

Director

Capacit'e Infraprojects Limited

HCC

Steiner India Limited

Praise For Author

Dr.L **R.Manjunatha**

Hi everyone,

I know, Er. Sonali. N from HCC days in Mumbai. She is a well-learned Quality control Engineer and an Excellent women leader. She has contributed a lot to QA -QC, and Construction management systems working with many organizations. Her New Book AQIQO is inspiring with insights, knowledge, and new ideas to the new age people.

She has narrated her years of experience in the field very simply and understanding to cvcryone in the book to make it more interesting.

AQIQO is what our young generations need to be smarter and better to achieve success. I congratulate her and wish her great success

Dr. L R.Manjunatha
Chairman
Indian concrete Institute-Bangalore

Praise For Author

Mr.Mahesh Malpathak

Hello friends,

I know Sonali right from my college days.

Always been an enthusiastic, energetic, and out of box thinker. Luckily a few years later got a chance to impanel her with British Standards, and the journey has continued since 2011 as an auditor, technical expert, friend, and philosopher.

Every meeting demonstrated her hunger for learning and developing new skillsets.

I am sure her first book, AQIQO, will be an excellent gift for me and all.

I wish her all the best for the same and many more to come!

Stay Safe,

Mahesh Malpathak

Business Head – BSI India West

Mobility Head - IMETA

India. Middle East. Turkey. Africa

www.ingramcontent.com/pod-product-compliance
Ingram Content Group UK Ltd.
Pitfield, Milton Keynes, MK11 3LW, UK
UKHW021926190726
13853UKWH00002B/863